TO DROWN A MAN

To Drown a Man

Tyler James Russell

TO DROWN A MAN
Copyright © 2020 Tyler James Russell
All Rights Reserved
Published by Unsolicited Press
Printed in the United States of America.
First Edition 2020.

No part of this book may be used or reproduced in any manner whatsoever without written permission except in the case of brief quotations embodied in critical articles or reviews.

Attention schools and businesses: for discounted copies on large orders, please contact the publisher directly. Books are brought to the trade by Ingram.

For information contact:
Unsolicited Press
Portland, Oregon
www.unsolicitedpress.com
orders@unsolicitedpress.com
619-354-8005

Cover Design: Kathryn Gerhardt
Editor: Bekah Stogner; S.R. Stewart
ISBN: 978-1-950730-47-6

For Cat, my Queen

with more of my love
and more of my gratitude
than you probably know

Poems

Gabriel	9
After	12
How To Hide	14
Ninebark	17
'Tis Said	19
When You Feel Fear	25
Consuming Fire	26
To Drown A Man	28
What You'd Rather Not Think	31
Pavilions Of Rain	33
My Great Uncle Comes To Repair Our Roof	35
To Kneel And Hug The Ground	37
Harold's Field	39
Taking Without Asking	41
Killing Spiders	43
Pinch, Burn	45
The Prophetess	46
Beautiful Fire	48
Birds, Landfill	50
Light	51
Rain On Stained Glass	53
Danse Sacree Et Danse Profane	54

Till We Have Bodies	55
Holy Ghost	56
Notes	60
About The Author	61
About The Press	62

GABRIEL

for my son, who died in utero December 2014

I wanted to say:
son,
learn this,
all things
you learn by doing
repeating
not knowing
by going
highyo
heya
all things
you learn by doing

I remember
your mother
a hollow tree
a sky
like aubergine
that sky

this time
carry me
this time
cover me
I remember
stumbling
highyo
heya
Gabriel,
carry me
and I will carry—
oh spirit,
I want to be
home

I remember
a hollow tree
and the sky
that sky

this time
carry me
spirit, son
until,
my son,
until
you start dancing

highyo
heya
be still,
my son,
until
you start
dancing

AFTER

the rain water
dries on the concrete
shapes nebulous
as relationships
from the deck I can
hear drops
like an IV from
the rooftop eaves
I woke up
rejuvenated
befouled
thin blot of sky
as if help might come
through like a hand
from behind the
curtain
to pick
me up and brush
dust from my ass

on all sides of our
property are
other houses

you can hear the
caged dogs
barking
but from the
deck I can see
only trees

HOW TO HIDE

A family hid for two years in a German attic
their neighbors shipped off in cattle cars
but the man who hid them did it so well that when he too
    was arrested,
no one was ever able
to get them out, so they stayed up there,
trapped, going crazy with being hid,
I mean,
they died

The only difference between imprisonment and hiding
is who shuts the door

Believe what you're saying,
then it doesn't feel like a lie,
keep your voice flat, look out
from the cave of your skull,
standing amid the bones
of the man you thought
you one day would be, but now
he's eaten,
because that's what you do
when you're starving

The secret to keeping someone
from knowing the truth about your soul is not to hide
    the truth,
but your soul
like when you must answer your wife,
her voice sandpapered
with worry

But when you go in looking for it, your soul,
the war finally over, you find it dead
slumped over the dining room table—
it begged air and food from you,
but you kept it safe, kept it hidden,
until it put a shotgun in its mouth,
because it can only take so much
for so long

Today I am an immigrant
from the country of dishonesty,
dirt-faced and newly-named,
ferried through a turnstile
to a home where I don't
speak the language,
know the customs
and where sometimes—
despite wanting *this* so badly I would
die to get here—

dreaming of the place
I used to know,
my tongue so easily grasps old language

Everything is foreign here,
everything an effort,
still I am heading up the stairs
no hint of life, but hoping
for resurrection

NINEBARK

One day, a shoot from the center
of your being will penetrate
bud, earth
into night air
into rain and invisible,
auditory birds

On your tenth birthday
you think it is only now
you have come alive, when
you discover
naked women, a rain-soaked magazine
here you write
what you've longed to hear echoing
in your body
and never been told

You think you
are the ninebark, burrowing
home
into dark earth

On your twentieth birthday
you dig secrets out
rip them into light
still clodded with earth
things you were never
meant to hold

On your twenty-eighth birthday
you will go bandy-
legged
the doctor
circumcising your strength
the violation of
his instruments
within you

But I see it happening, one day,
your eventual fullness,
breaking into clean air,
black leaves free, thankful,
holding rainwater
and sun

'TIS SAID

I.

The horses ate each other,
that when their king
was dead
the pair of them,
Iberians,
broke the doors
and answered that
primeval call,
a brain room never
thought to open,
a song they'd only
ever hummed

The chomp
the stamp
the sightless eye
the crowd that
presses in,
the groom
the bride
the king is dead

their mourning turns to
wrath

'Tis unnatural
to pierce my own
this flesh of flesh
(above the crowd
a stab
of color coming forth)

Is this starvation
or just a hunger misdirected,
like Jack
like Jill
who so desperately
wanted water?
But if the well was dry
if food were gone,
and in their absence
growing weary,
their teeth might grind
against the
natural use

(after all this time
your swallowed flesh
still will not digest)

Or did the one
decide to find
another king?
And did the other
realize
that she was leaving,
that what he thought would always be
was fast becoming *was,*
and in his lack
he grabbed for her with what he had—
his hands, his teeth
his claws?

Or was the king
and thus his death
knit somehow to their bones,
and when the bonds
were ripped
not gingerly
but quick
and cruel
then something else
too came undone

(as in my past
the ancient sin

which bleeds in every
cell)?

One of them
was first to bite,
like you first dared
to broach divorce
and mean it

But I was
just as desperate,
just as crazed
or mournful
and one
died first,
like Jack
who fell
and broke his crown,
but Jill
she fell
soon after

II.

But you have never
read *Macbeth*
and when you bought me
the play you loved
(the name escapes me now),
I pointed to
a waiting list,
the ones I'd yet to read,
my pile of ranking
preference

A chip on old linoleum,
where once I lost my temper,
a scar
for those
who next will haunt this home

If this is hunger,
I think about
the fish
the loaves
might we not
still wake to find
a cup of water

heaven's bread
where yesterday
was none?

You rub your face
and on your hand—
the sunken line
where once a ring
had bitten
into flesh

WHEN YOU FEEL FEAR

when you feel fear rising
in your throat
crowding out the vast landscape
of your soul
greet him as you would
an old friend
learn from what he has to say
listen
but not too much

then when he turns his back
stab the fucker in the soft spot
between his ribs
choke him
set him on fire
like a den of brumating snakes
and let the light show you the way

what is coming
is coming regardless
it's already on its way
we don't need a false messenger
to tell us

CONSUMING FIRE

You never know
the form it takes—
relentless love
never was
predictable

an ambulance
the aluminum so *real*
when parked
in your driveway
or a slow divorce
or maybe just the threat of it
maybe your father begins
to forget who you are

it could happen
when you lift your
hands
or when
the tech
wipes gel from
your wife's stomach
and says she's sorry

this boiling flame
this gasoline
a metaphor
for what,
God?

bit by bit
as surely as
magnetism
the dark
pulled
like venom
from where
my flesh
closed over

TO DROWN A MAN

who looks like you,
in deep water
you've got to mean it
he's going to get strong
once he realizes what you're doing
the fact that there is
nothing to hold
but a face
like yours, inherited nose,
recognizable scars,
presents further complexity
keep in mind—
you only have a moment
to get hold of him
don't have pity—he's
going to make the awful
sounds men make
when they start to die but
if you hesitate—

Don't hesitate

(a missionary couple found
an anaconda in their kitchen,
called a local
to cleave its head
but the snake,
as big around as you are,
turned to cut wire,
wrecked two windows
and a table,
the man, he's going to die like that)

He'll try to persuade you:
he's got a wife and kids,
and haven't you known each other
such a long time?
but that's the problem,
because while one of you
is laying bricks
the other comes behind
un-mortaring

The other problem
is keeping him underwater
he wants to float,
so you tether him
with cords of seaweed
that pulp apart

it will feel like you are choking a piece of yourself

But if you aren't ruthless,
he's going to be the one to walk away,
raise your kids,
make love to your wife
in the dark
if you aren't holding on
he'll kick off, not
for the surface,
but for you, because
I promise,
he means it

WHAT YOU'D RATHER NOT THINK

The grape vines woven through chain
link like the thought you came out here
to avoid, and as you pull it down rope
by rope you wish your brain was less entangled,
you try to think of your thoughts as cloud shadows,
like whales over the mountainside,
you yearn for structure,
order in the wild, but there are not
string cutters for your mind

Remember nothing
is final, one day this rectangle
may yield shade, a garden, but to tell yourself it waits on you
is vanity, look for lilacs,
the symmetry of sumac, collect
the weeds and bundle them
for burning, sever milkweed,
like you, filled with thoughts that
keep you out here when you ought to be inside,
but there are mirrors there, and here you cannot see
yourself

Move more slowly
than feels right, find
your blood, the inner voice,
things are exactly
as they should be
for now
yes, this
is how
you change
the course
of a river

PAVILIONS OF RAIN

When you wake and your hands
are swollen
you imagine your parents
dead in the other room
gun in your hands
and it was just a dream, just
the fever
but it was *your* mind that crafted it

I sat in the pavilion and the rain
fell like guitar strings
from the gutters
and what they played was a song
the beginning and end of which
was veiled
in eternity
Hallelu, hallelu
hallelu, hallelujah
praizshee the Lord
like this would do it, like this act
would be enough
to purge me clean

Who would I be if I hadn't polished
evil like a pair of shoes
and walked across
my life in them?

Come instead
to the river and bury
yourself in your failure
these are the nails
of grace and
you will see
truth in the water,
you will forgive yourself the things
you dreamed,
you will kick off your shoes
and run

My Great Uncle Comes to Repair Our Roof

He claims to have quit
but you can smell cigarettes
when he comes to the door
schlepping five gallon pails
like a boy
carrying buckets of sand

I escort him upstairs and he
crawls through the bedroom window
stepping out
onto canted shingle,
for months now, the sunroom
has leaked strings
of water I catch
in buckets

When he told the joke about
Congress and a condom
my daughter was standing beside me
I am afraid not just of heights

but the malevolent feeling
that something is willing us
down toward the edge

In my mind, rewinding
the rope of water is drawn
from its bucket
up through the ceiling,
his small frame re-compresses
and crawls back in
through our window
and retreats out the front door
into the past

TO KNEEL AND HUG THE GROUND

Sixteen years old and
my mother sees
her father's trifold wallet
full of dirt
when it opens
on the little metal tray
I imagine her scooping it into her palm
these few ounces
of the mound that buried him alive

Nineteen and
my aunt just married
when they get their pictures back
the figures bloom in water
her dad appears again
alive

They lift him from the earth
just to bury him again

Twenty-one and
my parents urge caution, waiting

Twenty-three and
I wear my grandfather's
Air-Force issued shades

Twenty-four and
I am always breaking sunglasses
leaving them on car roofs
smashing them underfoot,
his fall from my shirt
and a line of white
spears the lens

Twenty-six and
how the hell to raise a flame
on cheap kindling and grocery store logs
my son averting his eyes
like the sons of Noah
so as to not see my nakedness
my sputtering rage
flung like a bag of wood
across the yard

HAROLD'S FIELD

My grandfather worked
this field,
grew corn, I think,
but when I say *think*
I really mean *assume*
because I have no idea
I know he farmed—
corn seems logical

One time he mowed
my grandmother's lilies
the orange petals pulped
to brutal confetti,
bent stalks wet
with plant blood, then
she took a leg from his workbench
with a saw she'd never used before

This was his field, but
the dirt has run off, been re-soiled
your cells replace themselves
every seven years, I've heard, but
if we are being honest with each other,

that sounds convenient
Harold's field lay in this exact spot
though this one is not his
not really

So it is with you,
and all the things you did
but that were not, somehow
you, though you occupied identical space
cells replace themselves
like Roman legions
the rear guard coming forward
the front line stepping back,
like shark's teeth,
like when I, claiming "born again,"
claiming new identity,
tell you I am different,
becoming new, yet
afraid that we are both
as we have always been

TAKING WITHOUT ASKING

Stacks of newspapers threaten
like shattered buildings
but the table, I know

is not for eating
nor the living room
for living because

after August, you did
so little of both—
there are Bento boxes

on the bottom shelf
waiting and palely
fuzzed—like

Mom, you always
brought your own Tupperware
to dinner and ferreted

away leftovers
without asking,
as if taking what

we would have given
freely meant
something to you, like

the glasses I will
slip into a shirt pocket
before the others

arrive, not because
they're worth anything,
or because they were Harold's but
because I like the fit

KILLING SPIDERS

My father does a half-
laugh, inhaling spittle
from the corners of his mouth
whene he says something
of consequence, like he has
placed an envelope of cash
on the table, but is keeping
his hand on it, until he sees
you confirm it is the correct amount
I leave the endings of my sentences
incomplete, same reason

I was too afraid
to kill spiders,
I'd yell for Mom,
but I kept the yard looking like
a catalogue

The advice I repeated to myself
took twenty-six years
to be revealed for shit:
play it safe,

what you are already doing
is probably not enough

Once, I called her over
and the spider she hit
exploded into a thousand
infants that had been percolating
in her abdomen
now crawling for every
gap in my armor, my fear
that weakness indeed would show

It has taken much time, some
blood, but I am not the same—
my yard is overgrown, over-weeded,
but my wife is watered and known
and last month, when my kids
were spider-hysteric,
I stood, grabbed a broomhandle,
and took that motherfucker out

PINCH, BURN

Pinch and a burn, the doctor said, but it was more like the click of a door, like God unsnapping his bag and out rushed the universe—fully realized—the black still wet and hot like tonight. I tape cardboard over AC vents, trying to force coldness upstairs but some things you can't force, like when I wanted to know every detail of your past, but no matter how I seethed electric you would not tell, and it only made me want you more. There are so many things we cannot have, like I spent years wanting so badly to have my lines erased, to merge and belong, like now when I see my child and want, in some primordial center, to bite.

So long ago you—I mean God—told Abraham to cut his penis with a rock. By this you will know, he said. Know what? I still don't know. That something dark is cut away, that I am consecrated to you, like I wanted you to be consecrated to me, but we both have made mistakes.

It is raining. I will not be able to sleep, the heat, the storm, the shattering moments of light.

THE PROPHETESS

A thousand lives gone by
beneath this house
a dozen tried
and failed
to tame the land
I say "the" land
instead of "my"

And so with "my" wife
the prophetess
approach her with delicacy
reverence, you must
take off your shoes
(when I say you,
I mean only me)
drop whatever camouflage you think
you have—she will see
through you, will pierce
your heart

if you are not careful
you will look around and realize you are
off the property

and when she breaks,
she shatters,
the pieces
are named, they
speak,
but give nothing
to the knave,
you work
trust, you pull
ivy from the brick
with a surgeon's care

You have never heard her speak
as I have, her lips
a millimeter from your ear,
touched the corner of her jaw, seen
her heart betrayed
by her eyes

You can live in a city and not
know
you can walk this
land and not, until it chooses you,
breathe it into your soul

BEAUTIFUL FIRE

Early man slept in stone
and rock, wet innards
of the earth abiding and like him

I have known what it is to be cold
known what it is to see
un-looked-for fire descend your skies

You struck me like such tender lightning

Caught the bramble in my life
kindled stick and tree alike until—

You are so much light to me
others are only your shadow

One finger straining out of darkness
one world of another hesitant,
even to be saved, recoils
burnt, and I too have known
what it is to be afraid

I am quieted and tamed
by fire, watching, transfixed
learning to feed and nurture love

Forgive my clumsiness, my
awkward fear, but I am still
learning to handle lightning
still struck by
your beauty, your flame

BIRDS, LANDFILL

Before you can shut the windows,
a smell tentacles
through the AC vents
even before you mount the rise,
a mile away on route 15,
and worms toward
the back of your throat

shredded bags adorn the trees
in the air a hundred seagulls
mount helixes
sun-white
and I am wondering
what I should learn from this—

whether I, too, am drawn to that
which should be left behind,
or maybe this is beauty
in the least
of places

I am, as usual,
thinking mostly of myself

LIGHT

on Christmas, to remind myself

Tyler, yesterday you thought the world
was fifty-percent terrible,
and that was a good day,
today, you crept downstairs
with palpable dread about you
you mistake so much for darkness
when there is light everywhere
you see so much chaos
when a thousand years led to this

Make no mistake, it is often your eye,
not the world, that needs fixing
for every baby left in a car, there is one
listening to its mother's heart, for every
rape, there is a man who averts his eyes
from billboards, for every innocent broken
on the streets of Bethlehem, there came
a great and holy shattering

Tyler, all of time led to a night so many
mistook for darkness, but that night
in Bethlehem, the sun rose with thunder,

light moved in and never left, cracked
open like a book you bought and never thought
to read, cracked open
like an explosion of heaven
like the wall of air after a bomb,
so close your eyes and let the wind consume you

RAIN ON STAINED GLASS

We are draped in sweat
the unconditioned sanctuary,
the rain on the roof a galloping host
and the pastor says the word "community"
but I am looking at the woodwork, at
the stained glass of John Bunyon,
his panels shipped across the ocean

We are sweating in our skin,
the rain is falling harder now,
August wet,
through a shunted window-gap
it falls like static against a black pole,
goes invisible on the concrete

Again the pastor says, "community,"
he says, "transformed,"
as on the empty pew before me begins
a steady leak from three stories up
and I think of all the ways I try,
and fail, to keep you out

DANSE SACREE ET DANSE PROFANE

When Charlotte is sleeping
and my wife and the baby
are on the couch
and the sun is a spear
of white in the window
if I sit at the table in the kitchen
if I make a pot of coffee
and sit with my hands
open before me
light on the testamental words—

waiting looks like doing nothing

I remind myself that there are
creatures unknowable
who must cover their eyes
that the sky is a sea of glass,
and wait for a small fire to shatter
the roof, a meteor to split my kitchen table
to cover my hair in plaster dust

TILL WE HAVE BODIES

Everything rattles,
held so loosely
the skin
so easily parted
the blood
appearing like water
in wet sand

but one day
cells might lock
hands against
separation
the way our souls
will clasp
to you
or maybe
if they do allow
an inch
it will be
roses that well
from beneath
my flesh

HOLY GHOST

I.

You come upon me like a snakebite
that suddenly, and I'm speaking in tongues,
my throat so full of fire
my lungs unused to your breath
I speak often of your death
but have never actually watched a man die,
so the words come out bloodless

You come upon me, visceral
as a bloody fingerprint on my forehead
like my father trimming a maple with a hacksaw
all sinew, body odor
what I have been waiting so long for
like when, as a boy, after months of digging
prehistoric teeth finally came up
(or so I thought)
with the worms and calcite

You come upon me like not knowing
I've passed out
until I've already come to,

like seeing a knife sheathed
in my own flesh, realizing
that something is *in* you
Glory, I am bleeding
I am bleeding glory
You come upon me, and
my mouth is full of fire

say
my name
say something
say this:
I was twenty-five
my daughter's crib
a shadow-prison,
your spider-fingers over me
what you said that night when
it felt like I
might die

I look for hidden pockets
of your voice
the smallest wafer, but
secretly I am afraid
If I should find it—
what then?
secretly, I am afraid

of convincing myself
that my own thoughts
are you

The fossils I found
were not dinosaurs, but cow's teeth
my father had buried, and then showed me
where to dig one last crater
in our lunar yard
because I had expected them for so long,
he said

II.

Tyler, settle yourself
into silence,
take what package you find on your doorstep,
and serve it to the guests,
do not demand more—
more will come,
or not

There is space in the world,
the heron rises
shaking marsh water from its wings

you are a tree in wind
the universe flames
around you

Forgive your father
his false bones
you too have lied

NOTES

Line in "Pavilions of Rain" taken from "Judas, Flowering" by Andrew Hudgins

"when you feel fear" first appeared in *Phantom Kangaroo*

"Light" is after "Good Bones" by Maggie Smith & "How to be a Poet" by Wendell Berry

"Danse Sacre et Danse Profane" is after "Danse Russe" by William Carlos Williams

"Taking Without Asking" and "Holy Ghost" first appeared in *Riddle Fence*

"To kneel and hug the ground" is from Rumi

Line in "Beautiful Fire" adapted from "Marriage" by Wendell Berry

About the Author

Tyler James Russell lives in Pennsylvania with his wife Cat and their children. He is a graduate of the University of Pennsylvania and the University of British Columbia, and teaches English and Creative Writing. His work has appeared in *Riddle Fence, Apiary,* and *Inwood Indiana,* among other publications, and was a nominee for the 2011 Rhysling Award.

About the Press

Unsolicited Press is based in Portland, Oregon. The small publisher produces fiction, poetry, and nonfiction from award-winning authors. You can stay in touch with them on Twitter @unsolicitedpress & Instagram(@unsolicitedpress.

Learn more at www.unsolicitedpress.com.

www.ingramcontent.com/pod-product-compliance
Lightning Source LLC
Chambersburg PA
CBHW022014120526
44592CB00034B/949